T0324279

THE SORROWS OF EROS

THE SORROWS OF EROS
AND OTHER POEMS

by

HENRY WEINFIELD

UNIVERSITY OF NOTRE DAME PRESS

NOTRE DAME, INDIANA

© Henry Weinfield
Published 1999 in the United States by
University of Notre Dame Press
Notre Dame, Indiana 46556

Published in Europe by
Pieraldo Editore s.r.l.
Piazza della Libertà, 13/a
00192 Roma

Library of Congress Cataloging-in-Publication Data
Weinfield, Henry.
The sorrows of Eros and other poems / by Henry Weinfield
p.   cm.
ISBN 0-268-01766-2 (alk. paper)
I. Title.
PS3573.E395S57   1999
811'.54–dc21   98-42053
CIP

ACKNOWLEDGMENTS

Some of these poems have appeared in the following journals: *Colorado Quarterly, Denver Quarterly, The Forward, Newark Review, Paideuma, Poetry New York, Talisman.*

"Song for the In-Itself and For-Itself" was included in *The Best American Poetry* 1994, edited by A. R. Ammons (New York: Charles Scribner & Sons, 1994).

The section of the manuscript entitled Sonnets Elegiac and Satirical was published as a chapbook by House of Keys in 1982.

CONTENTS

ONE — SONNETS ELEGIAC
AND SATIRICAL

TWO — FABLES FROM THE
DARK AGES

THREE — BEAUTY AND THE
BEAST

ONE

SONNETS ELEGIAC
AND SATIRICAL

Letters to you, imprisoned in my heart,
Were never written lest that they be found.
I had to turn them into works of art,
And hide them in a crypt beneath the ground.
A sunken vessel can emit no sound
Upon the bottom of the ocean floor;
And I am shipwrecked, I am surely drowned,
Although you see me walking on the shore.
Letters to you must not be disinterred
Until Atlantis rises from the deep!
—Meanwhile we live in terror of the word,
Which cannot keep the secrets which we keep.
Our lives are buried and ambiguous—
If there were mermaids, they would weep for us.

Two

The park was where we found ourselves alone,
As if it always had been there for us
In some dimension where the sun shone
And we were naked and anonymous.
It was as if it always had been thus,
And always would be there for us to feel,
As if each moment were continuous—
And so it seemed, although it wasn't real.
It was the loveliest day of many a year,
The loveliest day of this dark century,
Almost too beautiful for us to fear
That we were taken in adultery.
The sun eclipsed the world, and it was dark;
And yet it shone for us that day inside the park.

THREE

Plato's Republic was no place for us—
We had no business in that perfect state;
For there the poet, deemed superfluous,
Was not admitted through the iron gate.
Republics must be kept inviolate
From those who hunger for the Beautiful:
You are too beautiful to contemplate,
And I am no philosopher at all.
The Golden Age could not be found in Greece
Without a detour through the land of truth:
Plato's Republic postulates police
To curb the anarchic power of sexual youth.
The borderguards have warned us, and we know
That we must leave, but have no place to go.

FOUR

Poets are liars, as the proverb runs,
And I, being one, attest that it is true.
Some lie for profit or possessions,
And some for lack of something else to do.
But I tell lies that I might lie with you,
Who otherwise were lost to me for sure:
If you were lost, no poems should ensue,
And this is what no poet can endure.
Perhaps you think it easy to devise
Fables to camouflage these lies of ours:
You need imagination to tell lies,
So Aristotle calls them metaphors.
Love lies, and the body dies, in grief—
Awash upon the shores of disbelief.

FIVE

At best, the poet's statements are absurd,
Or else abounding in tautologies:
The selfsame figure and the selfsame word
Can serve in satires or in elegies.
The poet tenders his apologies,
But says that he must manage as he can,
Which means occasional mythologies—
He is a poet, not an honest man.
But if you set the poet on a raft
Upon the sea of happenstance, admit
At least that he was true to his own craft:
There was a star, and so he followed it.
The star was distant and the craft was slow,
And where it beaconed he could never know.

Six

Heroic love, which yearns to be unique,
Despite the common mould in which it's cast,
Concocts a magic potion, so to speak,
To purge the future of its burdened past.
We know, of course we know, that what we taste
Is either fatal or ephemeral;
We know that nothing can be made to last,
That nothing lasts if it is beautiful.
What lasts is nothing, then; what lasts is death—
Death is where heroes make their last abode;
Death is the poison which gives love the faith,
With its last breath, to sing the *Liebestod*.
Embracing death, convinced that we are gods,
We sing forever—against all the odds.

Seven

The early Christians were so confident
That they could reconcile opposing views,
They turned the lamp that lit the Occident
Upon the darker wisdom of the Jews.
Their concept was that God could interfuse
The entire universe with His sole plan;
Omniscient and omnipotent, could choose
Miraculously to become a man.
But men are murderers, and all their art
The skin-stretched lampshade of idolatry.
—This bitter knowledge set the Jews apart
Through all their wanderings through history:
Their God was imageless; He had no name;
And though they prayed to Him, He never came.

Eight

An Irish boy was piping to a crowd,
As we were passing through a park arcade:
His face was so impervious and so proud,
As if he were the music that he played.
We had been talking of the Jews. You said
That those who were delivered to their doom
Restored the land for which their prophets prayed,
Where they were promised they would find a home.
I said that home is just a metaphor
For everything that we must leave behind:
There aren't any nations anymore
By which futurity can be defined.
Home is the hymn the angels play on high—
Upon the bagpipes of the Irish boy.

NINE

For years I called myself a communist,
But held myself above the common lot,
As if I had been chosen to exist
In lieu of those whom history forgot.
While others were anonymous, I thought
That as a communist I had a claim
To be the master whom his servant fought
For glory and the honor of a name.
To be anonymous—that sacred word
By many communists misunderstood—
I had to purge myself, and here record
That I was one among a multitude.
I was the beaten pavement of New York
On which you hurried on your way to work.

Ten

For years I sojourned in the Land of Prose;
With other sojourners I sojourned there.
It was a land of plenty, I suppose,
But in the end I was a sojourner.
I was a person then, a character,
And so I happened to encounter you.
It seemed that I had known you once somewhere,
Though both of us were merely passing through.
How long ago it was I cannot say
That I departed for the Land of Rhyme;
But it was long ago and far away,
And I am finished now with space and time.
When I arrived, I learned that I was dead—
And I am nothing now but what you read.

ELEVEN

You say that in these sonnets we exist
Not as ourselves but in *symbolic* terms:
No doubt you heard this from your analyst,
Who's paid to open up that can of worms.
No doubt the terms your analyst affirms
Corroborate reality, not art.
Reality, no doubt, is what conforms
To . . . here the syllogism falls apart.
Nature abhors a vacuum; in its place
Prefers that contradiction should prevail:
Either the world is all that is the case
Or nothing is, and none of it is real.
To heaven upraised or to perdition hurled—
Tertium non datur in this bitter world.

TWELVE

Your tourist-agent called it Paradise
—Meaning, of course, the weather would be fine;
The accommodations surely worth the price;
The food, delicious; the decor, divine.
—Meaning, of course, the West in its decline
Sloped gently downward to a sunlit sea,
Along whose beaches hedonistic swine
Groveled and groped for historicity.
—Meaning, of course, the wretched of the earth
Would shortly come to join them at the feast,
Impelled from where disease combined with dearth,
Beyond the sea, full circle to the East.
—Meaning, of course, you didn't have to choose:
So you enjoyed yourself, my shallow Muse.

Thirteen

Though Occam's Razor, the logician's knife,
Confined existence to a single source,
You took a brief vacation from your life
To find its essence in the craft of verse.
Meanwhile your life continued on a course
Which in your absence was beyond control:
Hurled by desire, that blind and brutal force,
You watched it grow more distant from your soul.
And when at last you fell upon your fate,
Was it a tragedy or merely farce?
Why were you always so unfortunate,
So prone to accidents, you horse's arse?
They clipped your wings? Well, now you're doing time—
For every verse, for every bloody rhyme.

TWO

FABLES FROM THE DARK AGES

An Essay on Violence

"But words of reason drop into the void . . ."
SIMONE WEIL, The Iliad; or, the Poem of Force

Who would have thought that what the sages taught
With such devotion would have gone for naught,
Forgotten in the coils of violence?

Who would have thought that it was all in vain,
That what was wrought would be torn down again,
That nothing would remain but violence?

Who in those distant ages would have thought
That repetition would be still our lot
And echoing laments of violence?

But words of reason drop into the void
And perish there, by violence destroyed,
In ever-widening pools of violence.

We are the playthings of that history,
The instruments of its dominion, we,
And gross materials of violence.

Subjects, we are subjected to the powers
Which have their being in not being ours,
And which we summon up in violence.

System gives way to system, class to class;
Mere transient forms, to nothingness they pass,
Suborning and suborned by violence.

Marx thought that with the bourgeoisie destroyed
True harmony at last would be enjoyed:
The consequence was merely violence.

Christ's admonition, "Turn the other cheek,"
Wrote Nietzsche, is the counsel of the weak:
Must we be martyrs, then, to violence?

And yet we know that to respond in kind
Is to succumb to forces that are blind
And cut both ways—the powers of violence.

Suffering, wrote Sophocles, can drive us mad;
Madness deprives us of what sight we had,
Conferring blessings upon violence.

Jihads, crusades . . . with labels such as these
We demonize our foes and thus appease
With sacrifice the gods of violence.

Whoever acts in concert with God's will
May abrogate His stricture not to kill:
It is not killing then or violence.

Whoever is the messenger of God
Need not forbear to shed a little blood:
The greater good requires violence.

"The highest wisdom and the primal love,"
Wrote Dante, are the attributes that drove
Our Maker to make Hell's eternal violence.

I beg to differ with the Florentine:
Your violence is yours and mine is mine.
It was not God conceived of violence.

God, if He but existed, would be good!
Would rid the world of evil, if He could,
The imagination of its violence.

He and His utmost seraphim on high
Are utterly unable, though they try,
To solve the antinomies of violence.

We are the ones from whom that seed is sown
And have to bear its burden on our own
And all alone face up to violence.

Read in these repetitions the lament
Reverberating through past ages spent
That we should do or suffer violence.

SEVERAL SONNETS ON THE SUBJECT OF SEX

I

Sex was a synonym for suffering
To that sad species whose perverted brain
Had given it language, without offering
A universe the language could explain.
The soul sought pleasure: pleasure led to pain,
And pain to efforts to obtain surcease,
Until the cycle recommenced again,
Either increasing or becoming less.
The animal inside you gasped for breath,
Beyond interpretation or belief,
As if the only point to life were death—
A long day's dying to augment our grief.
And all your vaunted language was in vain,
Lusting for what it never could obtain.

II

Sex was the solace of the citizen,
Who trod the dreary treadmill of despair,
Lost in the bowels of Leviathan
From nine to five each day and year by year.
Eaten by envy and consumed by care,
A shrunken monad of facticity,
He bore the burden of the character
The oligarchs conditioned him to be.
And on the *weekend* he would drive his car
Through mazes that the monster had made foul,
Or find some fellow traveller in a bar—
Some featherless biped thirsting for a soul—
With whom to share the momentary bliss
Of nothingness—escape from nothingness.

III

Sex was a serpent in the hissing glade
That held out promises of paradise,
Which we, being innocent, could not evade:
It tempted us—we ate, and paid the price.
The price, since nothing else would now suffice
But paradise, was loss of innocence.
Discovering paradise, we lost it twice—
In innocence and through experience.
The more we ate, the hungrier we grew,
Until it turned our hunger into food.
This was our knowledge, this was what we knew:
That all our knowledge does us little good—
Because we hunger and we don't know why
We live, we love, we suffer, and we die.

Reification and the Consciousness of the Poet

The knights of allegory hack down their gardens
lest truth be submerged in the Bower of Bliss
where the I says I love you only in imagination
and the individual no longer exists
but as a reification.

The I says I love you: the I, as a commodity
in the cycle of commodities, turns from the real
to mirror itself as a self-concealed mystery
and (under the aegis of the dominance of Capital)
vanish from history.

The mirroring self, fed on lotus and drowned
in the arms of the Sirens of its enemies,
discovers in vain what the phantoms confound:
that the Bower of Bliss full of sweet harmonies
is a Slough of Despond.

The phantoms unfold as the forms of the world
bereft of the future unravel the skein,
and as by the forces of entropy hurled,
unable to strive for perfection again,
the phantoms unfold.

The forces of entropy forged by the mind
beleaguer the fortress of its plenitude:
the epic is lost and the lyric consigned
to evil, as merely the absence of good
sings to the wind.

The epic is lost in the labor of years
as even the language is rendered obscure:
the garden dissolves in a whirlpool of tears
and the Palace of Art, which was built by the poor,
disappears.

The garden dissolves and the Bower of Bliss
except as a symbol of happiness
is a desert, a waste, and a wilderness:
ah happiness! ah holiness!
ah consciousness!

The Spirit of Utopia

I

The spirit of utopia is born in suffering:
There are no images of that pure world, because of which I sing.
Sometimes you seem to sojourn there in dreams or memories;
But all of these are allegories—there are no images
     of utopia, but only of the spirit of utopia.

The spirit of utopia is nurtured in denial:
Through building the great pyramids that rise along the Nile
As monuments to misery, you learn that you must wait;
For when you cry *Oh when? O Lord!* the sky responds *Not yet!*
     which is the motto of the spirit of utopia.

The spirit of utopia, dispirited and in vain,
Rains down in nostalgia on the cities of the plain.
In Sumer and in Babylon you reinvent desire
As shepherds in the pastoral come wading through the mire.
"Shepherds are honest people"; they do not need to sing—
Deadened by the deadness, the deadly deadening
     of utopia.

II

Hegel confuses harmony with history; he seeks
That beautiful illusion in the slave-states of the Greeks.
For whom are we harmonious? What slave shall read this page
At the end of Hegel's history, and dream of a Golden Age
    in which even the slaves lived in utopia?

Nor in the lap of luxury shall innocence imply
Playing at being a milkmaid in the gardens of Versailles;
Playing at being a milkmaid playing at being a queen,
Who had to learn the hard way—upon the guillotine
    (nicknamed "The Spirit of Utopia").

III

A traveler from utopia to these sad precincts finds
Most lives are lived in fantasies that undermine most minds;
Desire begotten by despair is blinded by deceit;
Bodies are bought and souls are sold on 42nd Street—
    and Hell is held to be utopia.

In Capetown and Johannesburg, when prisoners are condemned,
They all go to the gallows singing *Jerusalem:*
"Till we have built Jerusalem"—which now has arms for sale
To fascists in South Africa—and thereon hangs a tale.
Till we have built Jerusalem the poet spins out rhymes;
And yet he says the story's true: he read it in *The Times*—
    not in *The Spirit of Utopia*.

Chorus

The spirit of utopia is born in suffering:
There are no images of that pure world, because of which I sing.
Sometimes you seem to sojourn there in dreams or memories;
But all of these are allegories—there are no images
   of utopia, but only of the spirit of utopia.

On Syberberg's Version of *Parsifal* (and other post-modernist, post-humanist fantasies); Concluding with Two Lines from Jack Spicer

This is the myth of man before the Fall,
The myth of man before morality:
This is the modern myth of murderous man,
Before and after human history.

These are the poets who propound the myth,
Suffering from anomie and ennui:
They think *apocalypse* (it's always on their lips)
Will put an end to all their misery.

This is the holy fool who shot the swan,
Solely to vent his youthful energy;
He shot the swan, obedient to the sun,
And watched it falling from the neutral sky.

This is the end of us, very dear friends.
This is the end of us.

SONG FOR THE IN-ITSELF AND FOR-ITSELF

The in-itself and for-itself
Were two dimensions of the self.
The in-itself was satisfied
With any crust that fed its pride,
Hinging a self upon the pelf
Which it had smuggled to itself.

The for-itself, its opposite,
Burned with desires infinite;
Nor could it ever find repose,
Allow the boundaries to close
On any possibility.
Preferring anonymity,
It stared into a boundless gulf,
Forever searching for itself.

Like any Ghibelline or Guelf,
The in-itself arranged a self
In some proposed delineation—
A name, identity, or nation,
Accommodating to itself
The views of every other elf.

———

Meanwhile its counterpart knew all
The aphorisms of Pascal
By heart, and would reflect upon
Our penchant for delusion;
Our infinite capacity
For falsehood and duplicity;
Our vanity, profanity,
Habitual inhumanity;
How all our projects always tend
To come to nothing in the end,
Since what we are is more or less
Projected out of nothingness.
And so on and in similar vein
The for-itself would thus complain,
Abusing mankind for his folly
In litanies of melancholy.
But when the for-itself would rant,
Thinking itself still dominant,
The in-itself would softly creep
Into its bosom, lull it to sleep—
Until at length its griefs being told
The inconsolable was consoled
And a new cycle thus begun,
Though nothing new beneath the sun.

———

The in-itself and for-itself
Were two dimensions of the self.
This couplet chorus-like rehearses
The initial premise of these verses.
The self was bitterly divided
And each the other part derided,
With no abatement of their strife
Ensuing while they took in life—
And hence no way of putting closure
Upon our poem's paltry measure.
Enough! We'll leave them on the shelf,
The in-itself and for-itself.

That Sunburnt Pilgrim . . .

That sunburnt pilgrim whom you chanced to meet
In some suburban post-industrial street
Was Archimago, master of deceit.

Shading his brow, as from the burnished sky,
He slowly turned his head as you passed by,
And fixed you with a cold and jaundiced eye:

That eye, which millions have been ruined by,
Which is not living and yet cannot die,
Was fixed upon you in its vacancy.

Such was his lethargy, one might assume
He had been waiting there for you to come—
Another lemming rushing to his doom.

So, with a sweeping motion of his hand,
As if it all had long ago been planned,
He bade you follow at his mute command.

You had the power and might have chosen to refuse,
Knowing even then that it was all a ruse,
But did not choose to—or, chose not to choose.

You were as one who wanders and is whirled
Hither and yon, centrifugally hurled
Upon the margins of an alien world.

You walked through life like a somnambulist,
Impelled by forces you would not resist,
An easy prey for any hypnotist.

Yet Archimago, in whatever guise,
Is not substantial: he personifies
Our old, engrained propensity to lies.

His bargains are all struck upon condition
That only those who forfeit their volition
Shall be conducted to their own perdition.

Those dreamers who descend into the dream
Of their undoing are but as they seem
—This, in its essence, is his Faustian theme.

Yet Archimago has no power to move
The soul to plummet from its sphere above—
Except through some deficiency of love.

Our lives run counter-clockwise to the law
That Moses on Mount Sinai undertook
To give the people, though they fed the maw
Of Mammon and the righteous paths forsook.
It's all explained to us in that big book
We never read, whether from some dark flaw
Imprinted on us by the tooth and claw
Of nature, or because we cannot look
Upon ourselves without repugnance. Awe
Is what we do not wish to feel, the raw
Surge of the god within, what we can't brook.
Yet some there are that hold by hook or crook
The hope of paradise within their craw—
A paradise that no one ever saw.

Fables from the Dark Ages

"Also the Golden Age was a dark time
if there was one. I think it is now and was not
ever. It is dark now as it always was." WILLIAM BRONK

I

Out of the void, anterior to the world,
There grew a Tree, whose tendrils were entwined
Around the idea of love, whose branches curled
Around the idea of uncreated mind.
The Tree of Life was blossoming with fruit,
And God said *Eat thereof and be like God;*
But Adam cut the Tree down to the root
And trampled all its blossoms in the mud.
At which God wept and all the Angels grieved
To see their labor wantonly destroyed;
But Adam was a serpent, so he weaved
By devious turns his path back to the void.
—Which even Milton never understood:
Men hate themselves and blame themselves on God.

II

The darkness brooded on the frozen wastes
And mankind brooded on the wastes within,
Fearing themselves above the other beasts
Because they had destroyed what they had been.
Therefore Prometheus was named by Jove
To be a messenger between the realms
And bring man fire, which is the power of love.
The demiurge, descending, overwhelms
The darkness and restores the holy flame;
But having long been rendered impotent
By all that bitter history of shame,
It hurt their eyes! And that they might prevent
The god from opening their eyes to pain,
Once more they chain him to the rock; once more
They feed upon his liver out of spleen;
For they were vultures and they lived on war:
So all was done as it was done before,
And what shall be is what has always been.
At which Jove wept and all the Titans wailed
To see their messenger so cruelly slain,
Who brought man fire. Then the fire failed,

And all was darkness in the world again.
—Which even Shelley never understood:
Men hate themselves and blame themselves on God.

III

There was a man within the land of Uz
Whose name was Job. The same did Satan probe
To see if he were innocent; nor was
There any man more innocent than Job.
And on a day when Job had made a feast,
Sharing his bounty with his family,
Servants from north and south and west and east
Came bearing tidings of calamity.
One cried in horror that the Philistines
(Who, like the poor, are always to be found)
Had stolen the cattle and laid waste the vines
And burnt the dwelling places to the ground.
Another cried . . . and yet there is no need
To speak of evils that have long been known,
The things that Satan in his malice did
While going to and fro and up and down.
Suffice to say that in the interim,
Having now lost the fruit of all his toils
And all the children who were born to him,
Poor Job himself was visited with boils.
He took a shard to scrape himself withal,

And cursed his day and wished that he might die;
But though his sufferings were unbearable,
He still held fast to his integrity—
He neither blamed himself nor charged God foolishly.
And though his friends, his friends and neighbors spoke,
Blaming the victim for his miseries
(And hence originates the Jewish joke:
"With friends like these, one needs no enemies!"),
Yet Job himself, in spite of what he'd lost,
Neither blasphemed nor charged the Lord in vain:
A mortal man, he rendered up the ghost—
We shall not look upon his like again.
At which the Almighty and the Seraphim
And Cherubim lamented them full sore:
They could not bring his family back to him,
His lands and livestock they could not restore.
—Although the Bible tells us that they could:
Men hate themselves and blame themselves on God.

THREE

BEAUTY AND THE BEAST

To My Student, Colette, Who Wrote an Essay in Rhyme Royal, Complaining About Chaucer and Shakespeare

Colette, although I think I comprehend
Why some of Chaucer's *Canterbury Tales*
And Shakespeare's *Tempest* drive you round the bend,
Making you want to swear—or swear-off—males
(Because their heads, harder than those of nails,
Can never seem to get the message), yet
I can't entirely agree, Colette.

It's true Griselda and the Wife of Bath
Reflect a set of masculine conventions;
As opposites, they tread the self-same path—
Which leads us nowhere, as your essay mentions,
The road to Hell being paved with good intentions.
It's true that all of these dichotomies
Are part and parcel of the same disease.

It's true the tale the Wife tells of that rapist,
For all its moralizing, has in view
A fantasy egregiously escapist:
That men can have their cake and eat it too.
The ancient crone who aids him, it is true,
Conveniently becomes the lovely maid
He ravished—once he's promised that they'll wed.

And, yes, the gruesome sermon of the Clerk
Has something in it one would want to alter:
Griselda, face it, is a hopeless jerk
For being patient with that monster, Walter.
The analogy to Job would seem to falter
Upon a fact the Clerk has trouble seeing:
Walter plays God, but is a human being.

Alas! And is pure love beyond the reach
Of Ferdinand and Miranda? They betray
The rhetoric of slavery in their speech;
We hear it in the margins of the play
(For that fine insight, you deserve an "A").
Alas! alack! ah, woe! and well-a-day!
What are those lovers doing playing chess
On the enchanted island? It's a mess!

A mess, my dear, yes, history's a mess,
And power permeates the very pores
Of poetry—or penetrates, I guess.
It pours through language, through our metaphors,
And even through the soul when it implores
Deliverance from vanity and violence,
To be transported to enchanted islands.

There, on those yellow sands, perfection still
Eludes us, every man and every woman;
Yet Chaucer struggles, and he always will,
To find the perfect balance that is human.
Griselda and the Wife of Bath illumine
Each other's lacks and failings, it is true,
But also what Miranda keeps in view—
For whom all things are beautiful and new.

Variations on the Forest of Arden

Why are we brought to the Forest of Arden,
If there we must wander, in error, alone?
It seems to be almost (but isn't) the garden
To which we are born and from which we are thrown.
Why are we brought to the Forest of Arden?

Is it there that we ponder the penalty of Adam—
Tongues in the trees and sermons in the stones,
Books in the brooks—do they teach us to fathom
Why we always forget what we always have known?
Is it there that we ponder the penalty of Adam?

We hardly remember the Brother in Elysium,
The sojourning Sister, albeit our own,
Whose distance is echoed, as in diapason;
For to banish the Other is to banish the One.
We hardly remember the Brother in Elysium.

No artist of exile was ever so ardent
In giving us back to the things that we mourn:
The paths of the woodland at springtime are verdant,
The stars shine above—as they always have shone.
No artist of exile was ever so ardent.

In calling us back to the sound of the human
No artist of exile so sweetly has shown
What the mirroring stars in their courses illumine:
It's all there before us—and yet it is gone—
In calling us back to the sound of the human.

Why are we brought to the Forest of Arden?
Is it there that we ponder the penalty of Adam?
We hardly remember the Brother in Elysium.
No artist of exile was ever so ardent
In calling us back to the sound of the human.

Beauty and the Beast

". . . desires what it has not, the Beautiful!" SHELLEY, "The Sensitive Plant"

". . . the Orphic explanation of the earth, which is the sole task of the poet . . ."
MALLARMÉ, Letter to Verlaine (1883)

to Joyce

I

He met her in the Library
Where all things have their history
But nothing living may endure—
Among the dogs of literature.

In those lugubrious catacombs,
Shadowed by dark, portentous tomes,
She seemed a vision of delight
When first she gleamed upon his sight—

Or some such words to that effect,
Borrowed from some lost dialect
Which happy poets used to know
A hundred thousand years ago.

But how she happened to be hurled
Down to that Stygian netherworld
In which he spent his days in vain,
The Beast could never ascertain;

Unless (to invert the fable) she,
Playing Orpheus to his Eurydice,
Had braved the gloomy depths of night
To bring him back unto the light.

II

Beauty loved reality
In all its ambiguity:
She saw things as they really were,
Yet they were beautiful to her.

She lived so fully in the flow
Of being that the here-and-now
Was always dear to her and home
Was everywhere that she did roam.

That latter-day propensity
To anomie and ennui,
That strange disease of alienation
Had never marred her education.

Poetically she dwelt alone
In self-sufficiency, as one
Who hears within herself the song
We strive to hear our whole lives long.

III

The Beast detested the impure
Chaotic world which we endure:
He worshipped things celestial,
And thought all others bestial.

He with his telescope trained high
Upon impossibility
Would ruminate on human folly,
For he was prone to melancholy.

And oftentimes with clouded face
Would stare abstracted into space,
As if each solitary star
Could tell us who and what we are.

IV

This occupational condition,
Derived from frustrated ambition
And from the endemic narcissism
Of modern (or post-modern) ism,
Was a disorder that he shared
With many another would-be bard.

According to a certain gloom-
y thesis that Professor Bloom
Had recently set forth, the poet
Is driven, though he doesn't know it,

Not by eleemosynary
Motives—on the contrary—
But lust for power, or, if you'd rather,
Disguised designs to do in father,
Which makes him truculent and bitchy
(Thus Bloom—by way of Freud and Nietzsche).

Some diagnosed this diagnosis
As symptom of the same neurosis,

And some, more pessimistic, said
That all the poets now were dead.

Blizzards of prose and epidemics
Of deconstructionist polemics
Had turned them all to academics.

V

Here a hiatus intervenes.
Beauty is lost—and by no means
Will she be called upon to give
Her presence to his narrative.

Why should she languish as a slave
In some benighted poet's cave,
Or for an egoistic male
In Hades as a shadow dwell?
Let him be chained to his old haunts;
Apparently, that's what he wants.

Let him be wretched and forlorn,
By his infernal Furies torn:
We'll bring this fragment of his woes,
Though unconcluded, to a close.

With that, she rises up in flight,
Unmanifested, lost to sight,
Impalpable as wind . . .

VI

                    Not quite

VII

Calling these verses back to mind,
Years after they had been consigned
To an old notebook on the shelf,
Detritus of an abandoned self,
Musing upon the waste of years,
His eyes filled up with bitter tears.

Was it the first time he looked back
In terror that he lost the track,
Not even seeing she was gone?
How could he wander for so long
In error and have been so wrong?

But if the goal of his pursuit
Had been for a lost Absolute,
Maybe she'd never really been
Gone, but had merely gone unseen.

Maybe through all his wasted youth
Searching for Beauty, he'd found Truth;
Maybe that mania to transcend
Was ended and his tale could end.

———

THE SORROWS OF EROS

I

Eros would gather up the golden sheaves
Strewn on the path that rumination leaves
In ruins mouldering till the end of time.

This was a path where solitude was known
To every singularity as its own;
The many were as one alone in this.

He was a being; others were the same;
So much by way of kinship he could claim,
Kinship consisting here in otherness.

Among so many beings, being shone,
Held for a moment, hovered, then was gone:
Nothing for long could house or hold it in.

The glimmering world, the world beyond our ken—
That was a way to formulate it then,
Hallowed and hollowed out of emptiness.

Therefore the sages held it up to scorn,
Deeming it better not to have been born,
Since every form informed futility.

Life lives our life, the ancient poet said,
And ruthlessly each useless skin is shed:
The serpent only writhes to writhe again.

Such were the ruminations that were torn
From Eros early on a summer morn
Before the corn grown green against the sky.

II

Silence and solitude, oppressive pain
Of repetition with its old refrain,
In runes are graven on the human heart.

In runic letters not to be devised,
Inscrutable inscriptions are incised:
We come upon them sometimes in the dark.

The humus of the human, thick and deep,
Pulls heavily upon us as we sleep.
It covers us and closes up our eyes.

III

He sought the sources of the ancient springs,
The luminous and liquid solacings
That language proffers us against the void.

What if those glints upon the shifting stream,
Imputing depth to every common dream,
Were fatuous fires—a play of surfaces?

Or as the last philosopher had said,
What if those depths to which we thought they led
Revealed at last that nothing was concealed?

Would prosody protect them from the truth?
Romanticism was the dream of youth
Who thought that prosody protected them.

IV

Negative Capability . . . To cede
The initiative to words—a modest creed
The Enlightenment and skepticism spawned.

Syntax was certainty: to fathom sound
Until the plangency of sense was found
And luminescence glowed on simple speech.

How strange that in an instantaneous stroke
Uncanny combinations could evoke
The icy floes or melt the tears of things.

Speaker and spoken to were then undone:
Nobody knew, not ever, no, not one,
Whence it arose, that flowering into song.

Nobody ever knew the simplest thing!
Doubt that had flourished, withered, flourishing
Suspicion spun itself into a web.

What if the whole procedure were a slick
Conjuring trick of sophist rhetoric,
A sleight of hand beguiling and beguiled?

Syntax was certainty—and what it mined
Painstakingly, in faith, could be refined:
The craft was sure, however crude the ore.

V

In his perambulations round the lake
He sought contingency, both for the sake
Of what it was and what it might reveal.

Experience, thus, was to be cherished for
Itself and as a kind of metaphor
For what it pointed to but could not reach.

He led a life of allegory then,
Winged on the words that rose up through his pen,
Where what had been abstract was made concrete.

Sometimes a Great Blue Heron would appear,
Angling its elegance in morning air,
Always when one was least expecting it;

Or soaring oriole uplifted high,
Bright blotch of yellow blazoning the sky,
Gathered within the topmost branches' green.

Swans in their silence, simple and complex,
Beauty's enigma curved on slender necks,
Circled the surface, mirrored in the deep.

At other times desire found no surcease:
Nothing but common terns and hissing geese,
Or crows caw-cawing as in mockery.

Perpetual cardinals and painted jays,
Plumed though in glory, palled upon his gaze,
Familiarity disfiguring them.

Boredom, depression, stasis, ennui,
Modernity's prosaic progeny,
Flaunted their dismal feathers in disdain.

Shadows lengthened; it was growing late—
Which meant one had to be compassionate,
And bear the burden of the mystery.

And evening echoed the consoling dove,
Calling to mind Francesca's gentle love
And Mallarmé's great tombeau on Verlaine.

VI

The saddest quandary was how to live
Without the encumbrance of a narrative,
Complacent fiction or consoling lie.

Incessantly one sought the hidden laws
That secretly determined what one was,
As if one's fate were written in the stars.

And like a destiny the poem lay
Buried beneath the language, far away,
But waiting in its truth to be revealed.

One knew, of course, that nothing was the same
And never could be traced to whence it came
Through tangled passageways of origin.

One knew that being, being various,
Was arbitrary and fortuitous
In what it manifested or erased.

And in that knowledge one had grown resigned
To the abysses of a darkened mind
That tossed and plummeted in its own space.

(What proverb, precept or apt apothegm
Allayed such moments, being wrought from them?
Not to inflict on others one's own pain.)

Yet still one hungered for the Absolute,
Subordinating as if destitute
The green of summer, gold of autumn days.

And waiting for the waters to arise
Upon encrusted-thick velleities,
One spent one's time embellishing the myth:

Beauty is that which fills us with despair,
Authenticating by its presence there
The Orphic explanation of the earth.

The echoes still resounded, but the tale
From long-time telling had grown flat and stale,
Heavily weighted with ambivalence.

The ghosts of longing lingered on the shore.
—What if one didn't need them anymore?
Would they be dissipated in the mist?

Or, broken upon the rocks, bleeding and torn,
Naked as on the day that one was born,
Was one to be dismembered with the rest?

No one could say; no murmur from the Muse:
There seemed no point in probing for her views,
Which were, one knew, at variance from one's own.

Where could one go and what was there to find?
Nothing, perhaps, and nowhere; never mind:
In any case, at last one was alone.

Buried Beneath the Language . . .

Buried beneath the language, in the sea
Of all that deafens and deforms the ear,
The perfect poem pulsates—uselessly—
And yet somehow I know that it is there.
Is it some defect of my character
Or sad propensity the fates assign,
Some age-old failure I cannot but share
That always keeps me back from what is mine?
Or is it as the ancients understood,
For whom Apollo played upon the lyre:
Our apparatus simply is too crude
To process the perfection we desire.
One line escapes the roar of history:
You must be perfect to write poetry.

I.G.E.R. s.r.l.
Istituto Grafico Editoriale Romano
Via E. Q. Visconti, 11/b • 00192 Roma

PRINTED IN ITALY • 4 September 1999